MW00775530

Sincerity

The Essential Quality

Sincerity

The Essential Quality

By Shaikh Yusuf Al-Qaradawi
Translated & Adapted By MAS Youth

© 2006, 2008 MAS Youth and the Muslim American Society (MAS)
All rights reserved. No part of this publication may be reproduced, stored
in a retrieval system or transmitted in any form or by any means, electronic,
mechanical, photocopying, recording or otherwise, without the prior written
permission of MAS Youth.

First edition published 2007. Second edition 2008.

Cover template by Zaid Hisham
Cover art by Aridi Computer Graphics
Interior design by Michael Dyer
Printed in the U.S.A.

ISBN 978-0-9792113-5-5

MAS moves people and nurtures lifelong, God-centered agents of change. Our vision is a vibrant American Muslim community striving for a just and virtuous society.

Contents

A Word from MAS Youth

As Muslims, we believe that the Day of Judgment is true and that the Afterlife is true. On the Day of Judgment, Allah will judge our actions in this life. Then, we will settle in our final abode—either Paradise and joy or Hell-fire and punishment. How can we be among the winners on that ultimate Day?

The story of our existence begins with our father Adam, may peace be upon him. Allah taught Adam the names of everything and allowed him to dwell in Paradise. When the angels were commanded to bow down to Adam, Iblis[1] refused out of pride. "Grant me respite until the Day of Judgment," Iblis said. "And I will misguide all of his progeny, except for a few who believe."

Allah granted the respite that Iblis asked for, in order to test us. Iblis took an oath that he would invite humans to all that was evil, making evil seem beautiful and inviting in their eyes. He swore to prove that Adam and his progeny were unworthy of the pleasure of Allah. From that day, the competition between mankind and Iblis began.

Amidst this struggle against the whispers of Iblis, we forge our path in connecting ourselves to Allah. Our test in life is to learn and practice the divine guidance of Allah, while resisting the temptations of shaitan. In our hearts, we have a powerful shield that we can use against his whisperings.

That shield, sincerity to Allah, is the subject of this book.

Allah tells us about this shield in the Quran. Reflect on these verses:

We created man out of dried clay formed from dark mud.

The jinn We created before, from the fire of scorching wind.

1 The proper name of satan.

Your Lord said to the angels, 'I will create a mortal out of dried clay, formed from dark mud. When I have fashioned him and breathed My spirit into him, bow down before him,' and the angels all did so.

But not Iblis: he refused to bow down like the others.

God said, 'Iblis, why did you not bow down like the others?'

He answered, 'I will not bow to a mortal You created from dried clay, formed from dark mud.'

'Then get out from here,' said God. 'You are an outcast, rejected until the Day of Judgment.'

Iblis said, 'My Lord give me respite until the Day when they are raised from the dead.'

'You have respite,' said God, 'until the Day of the Appointed Time.'

Iblis then said to God, 'Because You have put me in the wrong, I will lure mankind on earth and put them in the wrong.'

" All except Your devoted, sincere servants."

"This [way of My sincere servants] is indeed a way that leads straight to Me," God said.

"For over My servants no power shall you have, except such as put themselves in the wrong and follow you."[2]

In these verses, we can see that Iblis recognizes that the servants who are devoted and sincere to Allah will be beyond his machinations.

---

2 The Quran, 15:26-42.

Devotion, dedication, and sincerity to Allah is the guard against the plots of Iblis and is the path towards connectedness with Allah and success in this life and the life to come.

The book before you is meant to remind young Muslims, those who are just starting out and those who have been active for some time, of an essential quality for every activist. Without the quality of devotion to Allah, the journey towards serving Him will start from the wrong base and will go astray. As we embark or continue on our journey towards connectedness to Allah, it is important that we start from the right base.

We in MAS Youth strive to devote ourselves and our deeds to Our Creator. We extend our hands to invite our fellow human beings to join hands with us, to dedicate our lives to Our Lord, to purify ourselves, and to devote our time, our money, and our intellect to bettering ourselves and our communities. I advise my fellow brothers and sisters to read and reflect on the book before you and keep it in the forefront of your journey towards Allah.

Hazem Said
MAS Youth President
December 2006

Introduction

In a letter addressing those dedicated to working for Islam, Hasan Al-Banna[1] outlined ten qualities by which an earnest Muslim could join the ranks of those who work for the sake of Allah. This concise letter describes concepts that are essential to the personality of the proactive Islamic worker. It is essential that we understand, reflect, and act upon these concepts. As Al-Banna said, "They are not lessons to be memorized, but principles to be put into action."

For this reason, scholars have written books explaining the ten principles in greater detail. The ten principles are understanding, sincerity, action, jihad[2], sacrifice, compliance, loyalty, resolve, brotherhood, and trust.

The second principle of sincerity is the subject of this work. Hasan Al-Banna wrote in his address,

> The second pillar is sincerity. Through this sincerity, the Muslim brother and sister should seek the pleasure of Allah in their speech, actions and jihad, without looking for material profit, status or worldly advancement of any sort. They should be soldiers seeking understanding and faith, not individuals seeking their own self-interest: ﴿Say: 'Truly, my prayer and my service of sacrifice, my life and my death, are all for Allah, the Cherisher of the Worlds.'﴾[3]

With this sincerity, the Muslim brother and sister will understand the meaning of their constant slogan—Allah is our aim, He is The Greatest, and to Him belongs all praise.

---

1 A 20th century Islamic revivalist who founded the Muslim Brotherhood in Egypt.
2 Jihad literally means struggle. In Islam, it refers to the internal struggle of self-improvement, as well as the external struggles of defending those who are oppressed, working for social welfare, and inviting others to the religion of Islam.
3 The Quran, 6:162.

Sincerity

The Essential Quality

Attaining Sincerity

Sincerity is to seek the pleasure of Allah through actions that are free from worldly impurities. The actions of a sincere Muslim are uncontaminated by desires; she does not seek status, wealth, popularity, or the esteem of any creation. When deeds are performed to win people's praise or to satisfy a petty desire, the heart becomes blind in essence. It is distracted by its desires and loses contact with Allah.

This cherished sincerity comes only as a fruit of complete dedication to the Creator, as expressed in the verse ⟨Verily You alone do we worship, and from You alone do we seek help.⟩[1] Riya'[2], the antithesis of sincerity, was considered a disastrous sin by the Prophet Muhammad and his companions. Shaddad ibn Aws, may Allah be pleased with him, said, "During the life of Prophet Muhammad, we used to consider riya' the lesser shirk"[3].

The Challenge of Sincerity

Cleansing actions from worldly desires and secondary motives is not an easy task. Sincerity is the triumph over selfishness and worldly inclinations, a feat that calls for more than just a passing effort. Besides

---

1 The Quran, 1:4.
2 Showing off and seeking the admiration of others.
3 Shirk means to associate partners in the worship of Allah.

purifying actions from riya' and corruption, the Muslim must constantly be on guard lest the shaitan[4] devise a new way to penetrate her heart.

Attaining sincerity is an accomplishment that has no worldly comparison. A righteous man was once asked, "What characteristic is most difficult for the soul to attain?"

"Sincerity," he answered. "For it gains nothing in this world."

"The most challenging thing in this world to attain is sincerity," said one of the scholars of Islam. "How many times have I chased riya' out of my heart only to have it reappear in a different guise?" Some scholars went even further to say, "Joy to the one who is able to take a single step forward, not desiring anything but the pleasure of Allah!"

There are some people who appear to work for Islam with a fervent, sincere vigor. You could not imagine, perhaps such a person could not imagine himself, that there would be any insincerity mixed with his actions. However, if you searched his heart, you would find that he seeks some benefit of worldly life in the guise of a religious worker. Or perhaps he earns no profit from his actions at the moment, but he yearns for the worldly gains tomorrow might bring.

Allah does not accept the actions of a distracted heart nor the defected work it fashions. He accepts only sincere actions directed entirely to Him.

The Benefits of Sincerity

In the Quran, Allah commands His servants to observe sincerity, especially in the verses revealed in Makkah. The Makkan verses refer often to sincerity because of their emphasis on the oneness of God,

---

4 The Arabic name for the devil or satan who tempts humans. In Islam, every individual is accountable for his own actions; the whisperings of satan are no excuse to be led astray.

correct belief, and firm devotion to Islamic objectives. Allah says in the Quran to Prophet Muhammad:

Verily, it is We Who have revealed the Book to you in Truth, so serve Allah, offering Him sincere devotion. Is it not to Allah that sincere devotion is due? [5]

Let us reflect on the following verses that demand sincerity of the believer. Allah said to His Messenger:

Say: 'It is Allah I serve, with my sincere (and exclusive) devotion. 'Serve what you will besides him.'... [6]

Say: 'Truly, my prayer, my life and my death, are all for Allah, the Cherisher of the Worlds.' No partner has He: this I am commanded and I am the first of those to bow to His Will. [7]

Who can be better in religion than one who submits his whole self to Allah, does good, and follows the way of Abraham the true in faith? [8]

...Whoever expects to meet his Lord, let him work righteousness, and, in the worship of his Lord, admit no one as partner. [9]

5 The Quran, 39:3, 4.
6 The Quran, 39:14, 15.
7 The Quran, 6:162, 163.
8 The Quran, 4:125.
9 The Quran, 18:110.

Criteria for Actions To be Accepted by Allah

Every righteous action must satisfy two conditions in order to be accepted by Allah:

1. It should be a sincere action with the correct intention.

2. It should be in accordance with the sunnah[10] and Islamic law, as derived from the Quran.

The first condition ensures the purity of the heart, which is hidden, and the second ensures the purity of the action itself, which is usually seen by others. This first condition of sincerity is explained in the saying of the Prophet♔, "Actions are but by intention and every man shall have but that which he intended."[11]

Thus, intentions determine the internal soundness of a righteous action. The second condition is identified in the hadith[12], "He who performs an act that is not in accordance with our religion will have it rejected."[13]

These two conditions for accepted actions are mentioned in several verses in the Quran:

◊ *Whoever submits his whole self to Allah, and is a doer of good, has grasped indeed the most trustworthy hand-hold.* ◊ [14]

◊ *Who can be better in religion than one who submits his whole self to Allah, and does good...* ◊ [15]

---

10 The example set by Prophet Muhammad.
11 Agreed upon.
12 A hadith is a saying of Prophet Muhammad♔. The sayings of Prophet Muhammad were meticulously documented and recorded during and after his death.
13 Muslim.
14 The Quran, 31:22.
15 The Quran, 4:125.

In the latter verse, "submitting the whole self to Allah" is to purify intentions for Him. The "one who does good"—the muhsin—is the one who strives to perfect the outer performance of his actions according to the sunnah of the Prophet ﷺ.

The scholar Al-Fudayl ibn Iyaadh illustrates the importance of both sincerity and correct performance in his explanation of the verse in the Quran, ﴾...that He may try which of you is best in deed...﴿ as follows:

> The 'best deeds' are the ones that are both the most sincere and correct." Someone asked Al-Fudayl, "O Abu Ali, what are the deeds that are most sincere and correct?" He answered, "A sincere action will not be accepted if it is not correct and a correct action will not be accepted if it is not sincere—it should be both sincere and correct. Sincerity means that the action is for Allah and correctness means that it is according to the sunnah." Then, Al-Fudayl read the verse: "...Whoever expects to meet his Lord, let him work righteousness, and, in the worship of his Lord, admit no one as a partner."[16]

We can learn from this explanation that sincere intentions are not enough: actions must also be performed according to the Quran and sunnah. Similarly, an action that is performed in perfect accordance with the Quran and sunnah is not accepted unless it is sincere and cleansed of all intentions other than for the sake of Allah.

Below are two examples that illustrate the importance of sincerity:

Building a mosque for a corrupted purpose. There is no doubt that the mosque is a vital cornerstone of the Muslim life; it is a house of worship, a school that spreads the teachings of Islam, and the social center of the Muslim community. Islam actively promotes the estab-

16 The Quran, 18:11.

lishment and maintenance of mosques, promising a generous reward to those who do so. The Prophet said, "Whoever establishes a mosque seeking the pleasure of Allah, Allah will build for him a house in Paradise."[17]

However, the hadith specifically mentions that only the one who seeks the pleasure of his Lord, not any one who builds a mosque, wins the prize. A mosque established with a corrupted intention is like an enduring blight for whoever built it. Evil intentions spoil good work and turn its fruit into blemishes.

Allah revealed verses in regard to a mosque built with mischievous intentions at the time of the Prophet. The verses confirmed that corrupt intentions destroy all goodness in actions—the foundation crumbles without the support of virtue and taqwa[18].

> *And there are those who put up a mosque by way of mischief and infidelity—to disunite the Believers—and in preparation for one who has warred against Allah and His messenger aforetime. They will indeed swear that their intention is nothing but good; but Allah declares that they are certainly liars.*[19]

Jihad[20] for the sake of other than Allah. Jihad for the sake of Allah is one of the finest actions that a Muslim can perform to bring himself closer to his Lord. In spite of this, even jihad is not accepted unless the intention is cleansed of all worldly distractions and impurities, such as seeking the admiration of people, showing off personal courage, or defending a tribe or country.

---

17 Agreed upon.
18 Being God-conscious, fearful, and filled with humility before Allah.
19 The Quran, 9:107.
20 Jihad literally means struggle. Jihad refers to the internal struggle for self-purification as well as the material struggle for justice, peace, and inviting to Islam.

It might happen that a person spends long hours in community projects and Islamic work, thinking that she is surely among the best in her dedication and commitment. However, it may be that her intention was not directed entirely towards Allah and was instead mixed with other objectives.

A man came to the Prophet☙ and asked him, "What of the man who fights for wealth and praise?"

"There is nothing for him," said the Prophet, repeating the sentence three times. Then he continued, "Allah does not accept actions except those that are sincere and purely for Him."

Allah says in a hadith qudsi[21], "I am the absolute self-sufficient, beyond all need of an associate. Whoever performs a deed for someone else's sake as well as Mine, I will leave him to the associate."

Mahmoud ibn Lubayd narrated that the Prophet☙ said, "The thing I fear for you the most is the minor shirk."

"O Messenger of Allah, what is minor shirk?" asked the companions.

"Riya'," answered the Prophet. "Allah will say on the Day of Resurrection when people are receiving their rewards, 'Go to those for whom you were showing off in the material world and seek your reward from them.'"

Ubayy ibn Ka'b related that the Messenger of Allah☙ said,

> Let the ummah rejoice with the promise of facility, brilliance, and loftiness in their religion, as well as strength on earth and victory. So whoever of them performs a deed of the Hereafter for the sake of this life, no share of it shall they get in the Hereafter.[22]

---

21 A saying of the Prophet in which he conveys something that Allah said.
22 Ahmad, Ibn Hibban in his collection of authentics.

These ahadith[23] indicate that merely directing part of the intention towards other than Allah is enough to nullify any reward that may have come from the action. Mixing sincere and insincere intentions occurs when a person seeks the pleasure of Allah while at the same time fulfilling some worldly motivation, such as gaining wealth, status, or serving the ego. Allah does not like partial actions and hearts that have any room for other than Him. As explained by Ibn Ataa' illah, a well-known scholar: "Allah does not accept a shared deed, and He does not draw nearer to a shared heart."

We can think of a number of ulterior motives that may creep into our intentions for Islamic work. We may not always recognize them for what they are. Perhaps being part of a group and working for a cause gives us a sense of self-importance and utility. Some personalities thrive on being active and busy—their ardor for Islamic activism may stem partly from fulfilling this need. Maybe we enjoy the spotlight that intermittently shines on budding activists. Others may find good friendships in the arena of Islamic work.

These are not necessarily negative side effects of Islamic work—some are the blessings of being part of a group that is working solely for the sake of Allah. And that is the key—your intention must remain firmly focused on Allah, despite any "perks" that may lure you on the way. While we may love the thrill of being busy and on the go or deeply value the company of our fellow workers, those should not become the motivations behind our participation. If we find the arena of Islamic work suddenly empty of close friends, behind-the-scenes, and tedious to our inner ego, we should still muster the sincere intentions that supply us with enthusiasm and a give-it-all-I've-got attitude. Allah must always be the foremost and only goal in our minds—wherever we can gain His pleasure, that's where we want to be.

23 Ahadith is the plural of hadith, a saying of the Prophet.

The reward of an action is lost when intentions are mixed. This complete loss of reward occurs when the two motives behind a person's action are equal: when she seeks worldly life and the Hereafter with the same eagerness. It is also obviously the case when she seeks a worldly objective more eagerly than the Hereafter.

On the other hand, when her motive to please Allah is greater than her worldly motive, we have a deep hope in the Grace of Allah that the deed will not be fully rejected. We hope that Allah, in His Mercy, will not totally deny the servant of all reward since the influence of the worldly desire on her heart was minimal. In this case, the insincere desire was not the motivating factor—had the worldly desire been out of reach, she would still have stepped forth to perform that good deed. Imam Al-Ghazali discussed this in his book, Al-Ihya' fi Ulum ad-Din, in the chapter of sincerity. Allah says, ⟨Allah is never unjust in the least degree. If there is any good performed, He doubles it and gives from His Own Presence a great reward.⟩[24]

This is our hope—that Allah may give us a partial reward if our intentions were mixed. However, it should not be forgotten that the apparent meaning of the aforementioned ahadith is that any deed not performed purely for the sake of Allah will be denied all reward. Hence, we should exercise the highest level of caution and fear in our intentions.

As for the one who seeks nothing more than to please other people or to gain some material benefit, not only does he receive no reward, but he invokes the punishment of Allah. He chose to turn away from his Creator, chasing instead after others. He made them equals to Allah, and brought about his own destruction.

In a hadith narrated by Abu Hurairah, we are told the story of three people who will be cast into Hell-fire on the Day of Judgment:

---

24 The Quran, 4:40.

the soldier who fights so that people might admire his courage, the scholar who seeks knowledge so that people praise him for his wisdom, and the wealthy person who gives charity so that people admire his generosity. Riya', showing off, destroyed the deeds of those three people and led them to Hell-fire. A similar lesson can be learned from the following verses:

> ⟨ *Those who desire the life of the present and its glitter — to them we shall pay the price of their deeds therein without diminution. They are those for whom there is nothing in the Hereafter but the Fire: vain are the designs they frame therein, and of no effect are the deeds that they do.* ⟩ [25]

An action that has no sincerity is like a barren field, a body without a soul. Allah wants the intention behind our actions more than the form. An action unaccompanied by sincerity is thrown back at its owner like counterfeit bills rejected by a banker. The Prophetﷺ said, "Allah does not look at your forms or appearance. Rather, He looks at what is in your hearts."[26] Allah also says in the Quran to the pilgrims who sacrifice during *Hajj*: ⟨ It is not the meat nor the blood [of the sacrifice] that reaches Allah: it is your piety that reaches Him. ⟩ [27]

Islam's strong emphasis on sincerity is not harsh or meaningless — life itself will not function nor reach for its lofty ideals without the actions of sincere people. The misery that afflicts people throughout the world is wrought by insincere individuals who do not care that they tread on the well-being of others, so long as their own happiness is secure. In pursuit of the meager enjoyments of the world, it does not bother them that they destroy lives, reduce build-

---

25 The Quran, 11:15, 16.
26 Muslim.
27 The Quran, 22:37.

ings to rubble, turn houses into graves, and life into death. Some good may be performed by philanthropists or famous people who want only some good press or a moment in the spotlight. Those who run after personal fame and status often do so at the expense of their neighbors and countrymen. Such individuals gain only a short-lived applause and the admiration of ignorant crowds.

Signs of Sincerity

Sincerity leaves an imprint on the personality and lifestyle of a Muslim. It affects the way she looks at herself and those around her. Described in this chapter are some of the signs of a sincere heart.

Avoiding Recognition

A sincere person avoids having her deeds and accomplishments broadcasted to other people. Such a person trusts that Allah accepts all actions, the secret and the public, and knows that the admiration of other people will not help her in front of Allah on the Day of Judgment.

Sometimes, avoiding prominence, status, and the community spotlight can be a greater sacrifice than abstaining from wealth and other desires. Imam Shihab Az-Zuhri said, "We have seen nothing renounced by fewer people than leadership. You would see a man who readily abandons the pleasures of food and wealth, but when he loses a position of leadership, he becomes angry and hostile."

Many of the pious scholars and righteous people feared that the charm of publicity and prominence would ruin their hearts and warned their students of its dangers. Descriptions of the dangers of fame and status are found in many of the early scholarly works, including Abul Qasim Al-Qushairi's *Risalah*, Abi Talib Al-Makki's *Qawt Al-Quloob*, and *Ihyaa' Uloom Ad-Din* by Al-Ghazali. Let us take note of the following stories and words of advice about the perils of enjoying people's attention and admiration.

"He who loves fame cannot be truthful to Allah," said Ibrahim Ibn Adham, a scholar known for his sincerity and renouncement of worldly pleasures. Although Ibrahim Ibn Adham was famous and lauded in his time, he found no pleasure in the admiration of people.

"I never found any delight in this world, except once," said Ibrahim Ibn Adham. "I had slept one night in a mosque in a village in Syria while I was suffering from stomach pains. The mosque's custodian came to me [not knowing who I was] and dragged me by my legs until he kicked me out of the mosque." Ibrahim Ibn Adham's joy came from the realization that the custodian did not recognize him, for no one would have treated a renowned scholar in such a manner.

In another story, we can see the companions' loathing of admiration. Sulaym ibn Handhala said, "A group of us followed Ubayy ibn Ka'b wherever he went. When Umar ibn Al Khattab saw us doing so, he hit Ubayy with his riding whip."

"What are you doing Amir Al-Mumineen?" we asked in alarm.

"This manner of following degrades the followers and is a temptation to the person being followed," said Umar. Such seemingly harmless gestures of admiration can have a damaging effect on the sincerity of both the admirers and the leader being followed.

Ibn Masud, one of the great companions, came out of his house one day to find a trail of people following him out of fascination.

"Why do you follow me?" he asked. "By Allah, if you knew what Allah has kept secret about me, hardly two of you would walk behind me." Al-Hasan once found a group of people walking behind him as well—he said to them, "Do you want anything? If not, this behavior is unbecoming to the heart of the believer."

Ibn Masud once advised,

> Be fountains of knowledge and lamps of guidance. Take to
> [the privacy of] your homes, be a bright torch at night, ear-
> nest with rejuvenated hearts and simple clothes. Be known
> to the dwellers of the sky, inconspicuous to the people of
> the earth.

And Al-Fudayl ibn Iyad, another great scholar of Islam, asked the
following,

> If you can be anonymous, do so readily. What is wrong with
> being unknown? What is wrong with being ignored by peo-
> ple if you are praised in the presence of Allah?"

These words of wisdom should not be misunderstood as an invita-
tion to isolation from people's company and disinterest in social af-
fairs. If you examine the lives of the scholars who spoke these words,
you will find that they were righteous public leaders and social activists! They earned livings for their family, knew the state of the society
they dwelled in, and could relate to people on a deep level. They
worked actively to improve the society around them and bring posi-
tive change to the lives of others. The previous words of advice were
meant only as a caution to believers of the effects of praise and rec-
ognition. In order to guard the heart's sincerity, an individual should
know well the hidden windows and cracks from which the shaitan will
try to enter.

Fame in and of itself is not scorned, for there is none more famous and praised than the Prophets of Allah, the righteous Caliphs,
and great Imams. It is rather the pursuit of fame and status that is
detested. If a person finds himself renowned and in a high position
without having sought it, then, as Imam Al-Ghazali said, "Fame and
status are only a trial for the weak heart, not the strong."

Self-Reproach

A sincere person always worries that he has not fulfilled his duty and that his shortcomings have taken him far from the company of Allah. There is no opportunity for self-satisfaction or arrogance to creep into the heart of such a person, because he constantly fears that his sins will not be forgiven and his deeds will not be accepted.

Many righteous people would weep incessantly on their deathbeds. They would be asked why they feared meeting Allah after all of the fasting, prayers, jihad, remembrance, hajj, and charity they performed.

"How do I know any of that will weigh anything on my scale on the Day of Judgment?" they would reply. "How do I know Allah has accepted anything from me? Allah says, ｛... Indeed it is from the righteous that Allah accepts.｝[1]"

The source of taqwa, God-consciousness, is only the heart. The Quran says, ｛...Such (honor) should come truly from piety of heart.｝[2] The Messenger of Allahﷺ said, "Taqwa is here ..." He repeated it three times, pointing to his heart.[3]

Aisha once asked the Prophet who was meant by the verse, ｛Those who give forth of what they give with their hearts full of fear because they will return to their Lord.｝

"Is the verse talking about the people who steal, fornicate or drink alcohol but still fear Allah?" she asked. "No, daughter of As-Siddiq," the Prophetﷺ responded. "The verse speaks about those who pray, fast, and spend in charity but they fear that Allah will not accept their deeds. It is these people who hasten in every good work and these who are foremost in their actions."[4]

1 The Quran, 5:27.
2 The Quran, 22:32.
3 Muslim on the authority of Ibn Umar.
4 Ahmad.

Cherish Hidden Actions

A sign of a sincere heart is to love hidden, inconspicuous deeds more than those surrounded by the allure of publicity and attention. Such an action, shrouded from the eyes of others but sincere for the sake of Allah, is like the foundation of a building—buried beneath the earth but essential to the stability of the entire structure. Without the foundation's strength, the walls would not stand and the ceiling would cave in. Even so, it is only the outer walls that receive the attention of onlookers. Shawqi, a famous 20th century poet, wrote,

> The foundations of buildings hide modestly,
> though they carry the walls and roofs with firmness.

Umar ibn Al-Khattab was once on his way to the masjid when he found Mu'adh ibn Jabal standing at the grave of the Messenger of Allah crying.

"Why are you crying?" Umar asked. Mu'adh replied, "I remembered a hadith I heard from the Prophet:

> Verily the most insignificant of riya' is shirk, and whoever opposes the friends of Allah has openly declared war against Allah ... Allah loves those who are pious, god-fearing, and hidden—those who, if they are absent are not missed and if they are present are not noticed. Their hearts are lamps of guidance that fill every dark, dusty corner with their light.[5]

Contentment as a Follower

The sincere individual works with the same vigor and enthusiasm whether her position is one of leadership or not. As long her actions are pleasing to Allah and helpful to the spread of Islam, she is satis-

---

5 Ibn Majah and Al-Baihaqi.

fied. She is not busy trying to attract the attention of other people or
running after positions of leadership. Perhaps, in her fear that she
would not fulfill the responsibilities of a leader, she prefers to be a
common soldier. Such a person does not seek out positions of power
and leadership. However, if they are given to her, she carries the bur-
den firmly and trusts in Allah.

The Prophetﷺ described this sort of person, saying,

> Joy to the servant who grasps the reins of his horse for the
> sake of Allah. With disheveled hair and dusty feet, it is the
> same to him whether he is in the rear or in the forefront.

May Allah also be pleased with Khalid Ibn Al-Waleed, the celebrat-
ed warrior and commander, who was removed from his commanding
post and replaced by Abu Ubaidah. Instead of resenting the demo-
tion, Khalid Ibn Al-Waleed served contentedly and earnestly as a
common soldier.

One Objective

A sincere heart is unconcerned with the opinion of other people—there is nothing attractive in an action that pleases other people but angers Allah. Striving to gain the approval of everyone is a
hopeless endeavor; people are created with different tastes, preferences, viewpoints, and goals. A poet once said:

> Who among us can please the likings of every soul,
> Between each soul and another are miles in between.

Another poet wrote:

> If I please the notables,
> The humble disapprove.
> And if I please the insignificant,
> The noteworthy turn away.

Sincerity frees a person from the stress and concern that results from trying to please everyone. Life is simplified because he yearns only to please Allah. His longing for Allah is captured by the following poem describing a sincere Muslim's relationship with Allah:

> Life is bitter — if only I could find sweetness with You,
> Rejection everywhere — if only You would be pleased.
> Even if my world crumbles
> that my bond with You would flourish.
> Knowing of Your love, all else becomes simple,
> For the earth is dust, and all on its face shall turn to dust.

Loving and Rejecting only for Allah's Sake

The sincere Muslim directs his love and anger only through the channels that Allah commands him to — anger and happiness, pain and satisfaction, proceeding or withholding is motivated by whatever pleases Allah, not by personal wants and preferences. Such a person cannot be compared to hypocrites who are pleased with the will of Allah only when they themselves gain some personal benefit. Allah says,

> ﴾ And among them are men who slander you in the matter of (the distribution of) the alms. If they are given part thereof, they are pleased, but if not, behold! They are indignant. ﴿[6]

Sometimes, when we are active in Islamic work we may quickly become angry or discouraged when someone offends us or hurts our feelings. Some of us may be so sensitive that we are dissuaded from participating in our work any further. However, a person who is sincere is determined to stay firm and remain focused on his goal, regardless of whether he is personally slighted or his feelings are hurt.

6 The Quran, 9:58.

He is working only for the sake of Allah, not for personal benefit or
the satisfaction of others.

Our mission of practicing Islam and spreading its message is not
the exclusive property of anyone nor is it the monopoly of a few community leaders. It is the responsibility of every individual. It is inappropriate for a believer to retreat because he took offense or because
of disagreement.

Endurance
The road is long, success takes its time, and working with others can
be difficult. The sincere Muslim endures all of this. The obstacles
he meets do not discourage him nor does he hasten the fruits of his
labor. Quitting halfway or taking a break are not options—he is not
working for the sake of victory itself, but rather for the sake of pleasing Allah in all circumstances.

A role model for such dedication is Prophet Nuh. He spent 950
years calling his people to worship Allah and succeeded with only a
handful of believers for his millennium of strife. He persevered in
his mission, varied his approach when it didn't work, and attempted
new strategies to reach the hearts of his people. The Quran relates
his story to us,

> ﴾ *He said: 'O my Lord! I have called to my People day and
> night. But my call only increases their flight [from the truth].
> And every time I have called to them, that You might for-
> give them, they only thrust their fingers into their ears, cover
> themselves up with their garments, grow obstinate, and give
> themselves up to arrogance.* ﴿ [7]

As nearly 40 generations passed him by, Prophet Nuh was ignored
and rejected by his people, though he wished only to guide them.

7 The Quran, 71:5-7.

However, he remained focused and steadfast in carrying out his mission.

The Quran gives us another example in Surah Al-Burooj of believers who sacrificed their lives for the sake of Allah, patiently enduring the burning flames they were thrown into as the disbelievers looked on. It did not matter to them what difficulty they suffered for the sake of Allah. They did not ask themselves, "Will sacrificing our lives really advance our cause in any way?" The believers knew that they were responsible for persevering, and that Allah was responsible for the end results. Perhaps their sacrifice was the seed from which new faith sprouted in the hearts of future generations!

When work is performed sincerely for the sake of Allah, it will be firm and consistent. The sincere person is sure that Allah is responsible for the results, which will come at the time and in the manner that He prescribes. Even if actions seem to produce no results, Allah will not ask people on the Day of Judgment, "Why did you not succeed?" Rather, He will ask, "Why did you not act?"

Open Arms

A sincere person is pleased whenever another qualified individual emerges and joins the ranks of the Islamic workers. He welcomes potential contributors with open arms. He gives everyone room to exercise their talents and play a role, without holding anyone back or feeling threatened and envious. Whenever he finds someone who can better assume a position, he gives it to him willingly and offers his support, content to take a step back and hand the torch to another.

Some Islamic workers, especially those in the public view, may cling to their position of leadership and fight anyone who challenges it. They will say, "This position was entrusted to me by Allah and I will not leave it to anyone else." They do not realize that times change and that someone who was once suited to lead may no longer be the most qualified. We often see this fault in rulers who refuse to let go of their stations, insisting decade after decade that they are the ones who can best man the helm and tend the sails. It would be unbecoming if the workers of Islam harbor the same characteristics as the rulers they criticize!

It is also inappropriate that Islamic workers use their role in Islamic work as a means of acquiring authority, as others have used patriotism and national unity. Shaitan lays many traps for the hearts of Islamic workers — those who fall into them may think they are serving Islam while they are really feeding their own hunger for status and worldly benefits.

So many organizations and movements have been assaulted with condemnation from the outside, discord from the inside, weakness, lack of motivation, and an unwillingness to try new things only because of the ambitions of a few controlling individuals. This type of leader refuses to change with the times—sometimes he burdens himself with more responsibility than he can carry, blocking the road for those workers behind him who have talent and youthful energy. Would that he allowed his burdens to be shared among other workers, whom, although they might lack in expertise, are willing to learn through experience. Qualities are earned only by working to gain them! By nurturing the abilities of those around us and giving them the opportunity to excel, we are tending to the future of Islam.

Sincerity in Islamic Work

Why is Sincerity essential to Islamic Work?
Working for the triumph of Islam and its return to the lives of people, complete with its laws, morals, and way of life, is worship on one hand and jihad on the other. It is essential that intentions are dedicated solely to Allah because an intention that is mixed with other desires spoils the action, stains the soul, and weakens the ranks of Islamic workers. In contrast, a sincere intention strengthens willpower, lights up the road, and makes obstacles seem minor.

Allah promises in the Quran that He will reconcile between disputing spouses if they truly desire peace, ❴…if they wish for peace, Allah will cause their reconciliation.❵[1] The previous verse emphasizes the importance of a pure intention when working to achieve a goal, because that is what will bring about the help of Allah. Salim Ibn Abdullah sent a letter of advice to Umar ibn Abd Al-Azeez in which he wrote: "Know that the help of Allah is offered in proportion to the purity of the intention." Thus, whatever an intention lacks in sincerity is how much the Help of Allah will be withheld.

1 The Quran, 4:35

Imam Al-Bukhari began his book *Al-Jami' As-Saheeh* with the hadith that scholars consider either one-third or one-fourth of the religion:

> Actions are but by intention and everyone shall have that which he intended. Thus he who migrated for Allah and His Messenger—his migration will be counted for Allah and His Messenger. He whose migration was to achieve some worldly benefit or to take some woman in marriage, his migration will be for whatever aim he migrated for.

In the explanation of this hadith, the scholars told us that a man emigrated to Madinah in order to marry a woman named Um Qays. The man was thereafter called "the migrant of Umm Qays" because it was known that his emigration was not for the sake of Allah.

The Muslim worker must delve into the corners of his heart to make sure that there is no flaw in his intentions. If he finds fault with his sincerity, then he should strive to purify his heart and to devote himself completely to Allah. The mother of Maryam[2], is an example of someone who devoted her actions completely to Allah. The Quran tells us her story,

> ﴿ *Behold! A woman of 'Imran said, 'O my Lord! I do dedicate to You what is in my womb completely to Your service [muharrara]. So accept this of me, for You hear and know all things.* ﴾[3]

The mother of Maryam used the word "muharrara," understanding that Allah only accepts the purest of actions.

Truth, justice, and goodness will not return to this world at the hands of people who work so that they may benefit from this world. Nor will such righteousness be restored by people who work so that others might admire them or for social status. Rather, truth, justice,

2 Mary, the mother of Prophet Jesus.
3 The Quran, 3:35

and goodness will come at the hands of sincere people, who prefer to give rather than take and to sacrifice rather than gain personal benefit.

Sincerity, the Crest of Islam's Soldiers

The true carriers of the message, the soldiers of justice, and inheritors of the Prophets are those who seek to please only Allah through their actions and look beyond any personal benefit. They are the people who will accompany the movement to its success, though they might be poor, weak, and unknown. Such people are mentioned in the hadith: "Perhaps a man who is disheveled and ignored upon entry is overlooked—but were he to call upon Allah, Allah would respond."[4]

Sa'd Ibn Abi Waqas, the great companion who accepted Islam early on and shared a blood-relationship with the Prophet, related that one day he felt superior to some of the other Companions. The Prophetﷺ, sensing this, turned to him and said, "It is by the supplication and sincerity of the weak that Allah will bring victory to Islam."

The Prophetﷺ was commanded to be patient and content with the humble, sincere people. He was ordered not to run after the popular personalities who have wealth and rank, who think that the dawah will be advanced through their abilities and status in society. Allah says in the Quran,

> ﴿ *And keep your soul content with those who call on their Lord morning and evening, seeking His Face; and let not your eyes pass beyond them, seeking the pomp and glitter of this life; nor obey any whose heart We have permitted to neglect the remembrance of Allah—one who follows his own desires and whose case has gone beyond all bounds.* ﴾[5]

4 Muslim.
5 The Quran, 11:28.

A person who works sincerely for the sake of Allah is not tempted by the lures of worldly prominence. The world is not his biggest worry or interest; in fact, it does not weigh much more in his eyes than the wing of a fly. His sole desire is that Allah includes him among the righteous, committed, and successful soldiers of Islam. This goal should be clear to all those who work for the return of Islam. While the landmarks along the journey might be an Islamic state, a new civilization, or a Muslim society, the ultimate objective of every Islamic worker is one and only one: to win the pleasure and reward of Allah.

Beware the False Front
In the midst of the Islamic workers, there are individuals who behave like parasites in a healthy body. These intruders use the movement as a personal vehicle to their own ambitions. A bystander would think them well-meaning, dedicated individuals—their words are sweet and their appearances charismatic. However, their hearts are empty of all but their desires. They are a people who the Messenger of Allah described in a hadith:

> There will come at the end of time men who will deceive the world—they will wear clothes of sheepskin and their words will seem sweeter than honey, but their hearts will be the hearts of wolves. Allah will say, 'Are you deluded or do you brazenly defy me? I swear by Myself to afflict them with a calamity that will leave the wise bewildered.

Two Groups
The Messenger of Allah divided people into two types. The first is a person who lives for herself and her desires—a slave of wealth and worldly splendor. If her goals are achieved, she is pleased, and if she is deprived, she is angry, hopeless, and depressed. The second type

of person one who lives for the truth, prepared to sacrifice whatever needed, expecting no worldly payment or status. She works productively without attracting attention to herself.

Portraits of these two contrasting individuals are painted in the following hadith,

> Perish the slave of the dinar, dirham,[6] qatifah[7], and khamisah[8] for if he is given, he is pleased—otherwise he is dissatisfied! Joy to the slave who grasps the reins of his horse for the sake of Allah! With disheveled hair and dusty feet, it is the same to him whether he is in the rear or in the forefront.[9]

6 Early Arab units of currency.
7 An expensive, soft fabric.
8 A luxurious garment.
9 Bukhari.

The Fruits of Sincerity

Sincerity brings with it gifts that revitalize and soothe the soul. A few of them are described in this chapter.

Inner Tranquility

A sincere Muslim is at peace with herself—her heart is at ease and her mind is composed. Her heart is neither anxious nor divided between opposing objectives because her purpose is only to please her Creator. Such clarity of vision relieves the soul from the stress of worrying about the opinions of others and choosing between divergent pathways. So much purpose and peace of mind lies in the one who is able to block out all of these distractions—the nerve-racking diversions that trouble so many others do not worry her, for she has but one harmonious, cohesive aspiration.

Allah described the sincere believer as a devoted servant who knows what pleases and angers his master, and thus commits his entire life to gratifying his master and doing what is beloved to him. On the contrary, a disbeliever is like a servant who answers to several querulous masters, each of them commanding contradicting orders. This servant's mind is overwhelmed and his heart is torn. Allah says in the Quran:

*❨Allah puts forth a parable: a man belonging to many partners
at variance with each other, and a man belonging entirely to
one master. Are those two equal in comparison? Praise be to
Allah! But most people have no knowledge.❩* [1]

Willpower

Sincerity gives the soul a tremendous store of endurance and strength,
which springs directly from the loftiness of its purpose: the pleasure
and reward of Allah. A person who seeks wealth, status, or power is
crippled when the prospects for reaching his prize dim. He grovels in
front of those who are able to give him what he wants and is helpless
when the prize slips through his hands.

On the other hand, a person who serves Allah is connected to an
energy source that never diminishes. His commitment and sincerity give him more strength than any worldly provision. The sincere
Muslim is not tempted by false promises and does not long for what
people offer him. He is not driven by his desires nor immobilized by
fear.

His model is the Prophet Muhammad☙ who, when he was offered
power, status, and wealth, answered resolutely,

> By Allah, if they put the sun in my right hand and the
> moon in my left so that I leave this matter, I would not
> leave it until Allah directs me or I perish upon it.

If the Prophet☙ had the faintest inclination towards wealth or
power, he would have given in to their offers. However, he knew his
goal and devoted himself to it. The willpower of the Prophet in carrying out his mission stands out time and again throughout his life.

1 The Quran, 39:29.

Commitment

Among the fruits of sincerity is persistent, consistent, and steady action. When the objective is to please other people or to satisfy some desire, actions are suspended whenever people are not around or a desire is unattainable. When the motivation behind an action disappears, any further effort becomes tedious and pointless.

However, the one who strives purely for Allah will not slacken or become disheartened because the One for whom he works is always with him, always present. The Face of Allah will be there even when the faces of humanity are turned away or absent. Allah says in the Quran, ⟨Everything that exists will perish except His Own Face. To Him belongs the Command, and to Him will you all be brought back.⟩[2]

This is why the pious have said, "Whatever is for Allah will be steady and constant, and whatever is for other than Allah will be broken and irregular." Indeed, this is what we see with our own eyes and experience in our lifetimes. It will continue to be a paradigm that plays out in all places at all times.

An Entire Life of Worship

Sincerity is like a magic ingredient: added to any action, it transforms the action into an act of worship endearing to Allah. It transforms everyday tasks and permissible actions into worship. The Prophet ﷺ described turning the everyday task of feeding your family into worship,

> You do not spend anything seeking the pleasure of Allah except that it is counted as charity—even the morsel of food that you put in the mouth of your wife.[3]

2 The Quran, 28:88.
3 Agreed upon.

Allah described those who responded to the call to fight for
His sake,

> ❴ ...Because nothing could they suffer or do, but was reckoned
> to their credit as a deed of righteousness in the Cause of Allah,
> whether they suffered thirst, fatigue, hunger; trod paths to
> raise the ire of the Unbelievers or received any injury whatever
> from an enemy. For Allah does not suffer the reward to be lost
> of those who do good. Nor could they spend anything for the
> cause — small or great — nor trek across a valley but the deed
> is inscribed to their credit, that Allah may return their deed
> with the best possible reward. ❵ 4

Their sensations of hunger and thirst, marching, and spending all
registered as good deeds with Allah, so long as their intention was for
His sake.

Also among the blessings and gifts of sincerity is that the sincere
person can receive the full reward of actions he was unable to complete. Allah describes the reward of one who migrates for the sake
of Allah, but is unable to complete his migration. Such a person still
receives the full reward of migration, because of his intention and
sincerity,

> ❴ ...Whoever leaves his home, migrating for the cause of Allah
> and His Messenger, and death overtakes him, his reward be-
> comes due and sure with Allah, for Allah is Oft-Forgiving,
> Most Merciful. ❵ 5

In fact, the sincere Muslim can reap the full reward of actions he
never even performed. Many ahadith confirm that this is possible.
Anas ibn Maalik narrated, "While we were returning from the Battle

4 The Quran, 9:120.
5 The Quran, 4:100.

of Tabuk, the Prophet of Allah said,

> There are people who stayed behind in Madinah. We did not trek a mountain path nor cross a valley except that they were with us. They were only held back by a [valid] excuse.[6]

In another hadith the Messenger of Allah said,

> Whoever goes to sleep at night with the intention to pray the night prayer later on, but was overcome with sleep until the morning, his intention to pray will be recorded and his sleep is a gift for him from his Lord.[7]

Sometimes, a sincere Muslim will try to complete an action, but will make a mistake in its performance. Because of his sincerity, however, the intention will intercede on his behalf, compensating for the error or deficiency. Another hadith tells the story of a man who gave charity three nights in a row. Unknowingly, he gave his money one night to a thief, the next night to a prostitute, and the third night to a wealthy man. When he discovered his mistake, he praised Allah and shrugged off his disappointment.

Yet Allah would further relieve the man's heart. That night, the man saw in his dream someone who told him, "The charity you gave to the thief might persuade him to abandon thievery. The charity you gave to the prostitute might persuade her to abandon adultery. And as for the wealthy man, the charity you gave him might encourage him to give more for the sake of Allah."[8]

Allah accepted his charity and did not decrease from its value or importance in this life or the next. Indeed, that is the reward of the sincere.

6 Bukhari.
7 An-Nasaai, Ibn Majah.
8 Bukhari.

Conclusion

The challenge of maintaining sincerity in your heart will grip you for your entire life. How amazing the human soul—that an intention makes a world of difference, though actions may be identical on the outside. Every supplication and every moment alone with the Creator you pray that you are counted among the sincere ones. The pursuit of sincerity is a lifelong journey, and your willpower must be sustained and renewed if you are to make it safely to the finish line.

After reading about how even the greatest believers struggled to purify their intentions, some may feel disheartened. After all, if the likes of Umar Ibn Al-Khattab and Mu'adh ibn Jabal struggled with sincerity, how difficult will it be for us? Yet this short work was designed to motivate the young Islamic worker, not to discourage him. If we feel frustration at such a reminder, we must work to restore our hope in Allah. Never forget—despite the long road ahead and the continuous effort required—that Allah would never put before you a challenge that you cannot handle.

All around you, at your very fingertips, are tools to help you build and maintain sincerity. The five prayers, our daily meetings with the Quran, and the acts of worship that we perform everyday are checkpoints for our level of sincerity. Ask yourself, is this prostration affecting my heart? Do these verses strike a chord in me? Am I acting upon what I learn? Is my participation in this committee for the sake of Allah, or for some other personal fulfillment?

When we realize how far we are from an ideal, it does not mean there is no hope. It does not mean we are bad people or that our environment has ruined all of our chances. It only means there is work to be done. Indeed, there is always work to be done.

That realization should be an awakening and a call to action. As you roll up your sleeves, you will be taking one step towards the Creator. And the Messenger told us that Allah said, "…If my servant comes to me walking, I come to him running."[1]

There is no limit to the heights to which sincerity can soar, nor an end to the struggle of rooting sincerity in the heart. Whether you are just starting out in your relationship with Allah or have been practicing for many years, sincerity is a goal for which every Muslim must strive.

The companionship of righteous peers who will remind you of your duties to Allah is indispensable. Gatherings in which Allah is remembered can bring sensitivity to your heart and tears to your eyes. In almost every major U.S. city, MAS Youth offers programs and services, such as the MAS Youth Usrah Program and the nationwide Tarbiyah & Ilm camps, that offer guidance, structure, and inspiration for the young American struggling to discover and strengthen her connection with the Creator.

---

1 Excerpt from a hadith qudsi authenticated by Bukhari and Muslim.

Translators' Note

Sincerity, The Essential Quality is an adapted translation of Shaikh Yusuf Al-Qaradawi's *Hawla Rukn Al-Ikhlas.* In this concise work, Shaikh Al-Qaradawi addresses a most crucial element for the success of our Islamic work in the United States.

This is an adapted translation, which means that in some places we attempted to adapt the original Arabic text to be relevant to an American context. Some verses and ahadith were translated in a manner that we hope best captured the meaning of the text, instead of a strictly literal rendition of the words.

The use of Arabic words in the translation was limited to instances when there was either no English equivalent or the English explanation was lengthy. In such cases, we used the Arabic term for convenience. The explanatory footnotes will help readers who are unfamiliar with basic Islamic terminology.

In Arabic, the pronoun 'he' often refers to both genders. In an effort to convey that meaning in English, the text regularly alternates the use of 'he' and 'she.'

We ask Allah to forgive all of our mistakes and shortcomings in this work.

Maha Ezzeddine &
MAS Youth Editing Team
December 2006

Made in the USA
Coppell, TX
26 September 2024

37749131R00038